Flammable, Inflammable

Flammable, Inflammable

Selected Poems 1991–2006

Greg Darms

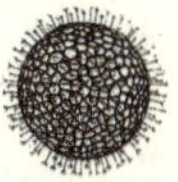

Radiolarian Press, Astoria, Oregon

Radiolarian Press
92643 John Day River Road
Astoria, Oregon 97103

First Edition

Grateful acknowledgement is made to the following publications in which some of these poems first appeared, sometimes in earlier versions:

Barnabe Mountain Review, Bellowing Ark, Black Hills Audubon Society, Canary Creek Review, convolvulus, Entelechy, Exit 13, Estero, Fish Dance, High Desert Journal, HipFish, Isotope, Limestone, Northwest Poets and Artists Calendar, The Pacific Sun, The Portland Oregonian, Prairie Fire, The Saint Ann's Review, Square Lake, Volt, Wild Earth. "In the Last Oak Meadows" was also excerpted in *The Butterflies of Cascadia.*

ISBN 1–887853–22–7

To the memory of my mother and my father.

Eppur si muove.

Table of Contents

1 *hope of hawk*

2 *town dog*

4 *the acquistorium*

5 *knot*

1

hope of hawk

What infinite leisure it requires...to appreciate a single phenomenon! You must camp down beside it as if for life...

Henry David Thoreau,
Journal, Dec. 28, 1852

Evening, Soleduck River

What light gave is lost.
Contour of deadfall,

cedar and spruce, salal and rose
fall and fade. Stumble

in elk wallow, trip
through slide alder,

lose it all, find
rock under rocks,

devil's club, fairy bells.
Stop in the trail

by riffle, in clearing.
Listen to gossip

behind moss curtains.
Taste the river night.

Velella

High on the beach
I found a glass float
after a glass-float thought
(blue)
in a drift of little blue sails

then the moon
precisely
from behind a hint of clouds
found me.

Storm from the Sea

A cloud opened when you blew out the candle.
You made a soft sound when the rain hit the glass.

Storm and storm and storm passed over our island.
In the morning a fish, cold and clear-eyed,

lay behind a chair. You gave me counsel
to wrap it in wet, to open the window, to let it go.

All day we swim out with flying fish
into the world that contains each other.

Ornithology

1

This little empty morning
a golden-crowned sparrow
breathing north
let three notes fall.

In hearing, I was stilled,
had to see and to see
stepped from cover,
lifted my eyes

so the singing stopped.
We faced. Silence
struck the space between.
The notes still rang.

When pulse stirred
the binding lull
I moved
one step.

Three notes
again, again,
like leaves falling
through mind, keening

not for me. They railed
wordless beyond care
and dared the sky to join.
I add the words.

2

Following a red-eyed vireo
        into weeping willow nightshade
                I – *psst! psst!*
                        to attract
                        what? –
                        find

        Cooper's hawk with sparrow
                in grip
                unblinking
                        rip
                        feathers out
                taking meat
                bowing
                and taking.

        Back
        by the trail
                waxwings pick at
                blackberries
                        finches tear at
                        thistles

        I nibble
                on this world.

Study

A Present must be invented that will not stop presenting itself.
Hélène Cixous

Things fill my study,
sometimes seem to glow. My father's reel,
a rusting *Ocean Spinner,*

is wound with line that predates mono-fil.
I keep it on a shelf
with photos: me, a beach, with a book, clouds.

Kuan-Yin, a lizard, my family
reach across the room. Unseen they come
to mind. When I sit to write

the cat lies on my paper, licks her paw,
stops to listen. A wren
beyond the window flicks its tail within

the focussed frame. Heart and
eyes are empty but for all that enters
knowing, not to know.

A Photograph

for DJD

An old Yashica two-and-a-quarter
look-through-the-top ground glass
twin lens reflex; hand-held light
meter; I set the exposure, chose
the depth I could afford, aimed,
and framed, and focussed. Then
I gave the box to my brother's boy
and told him to get us in the middle
and press the button. My arm around
my brother's shoulders, his arm
I helped lift to put around mine.
We had played a bit of tennis.
He was feeling good, and the oaks
in his Orangevale yard were rich
with the spring before the drought.
I was using Ilford 400, black and
white, I was aware of the Zone
System and I knew what I wanted
in a negative.
When I saw the image
emerge in the bath in the red light
he was already in the last stages
of chemo. We were both smiling.
There were many tones of grey,
some white and more than enough
black. The oaks were as clear as
our eyes. We were perfectly centered.

Remains

I saw the black flies first,
slow, huge, vibrating
on the sand, then
black leather straps
the spring tide flood
had uncovered, white
splinters and whole bones
and the smell
spreading inland
by cut stumps of fir
uprooted, scattered
on that spit where we walked
by the estero. With the vultures
then I knew the thing

and I remembered
the screech owl I had moved
from the road
ear tufts laid back flat
one eye hemorrhaged
a spot of blood
the leading wing feather
minutely ribbed
and infinitely laced
I could feel falling
into that world,
the quiet plunge
through black branches

to a soft place
under cedar.

When I called to my father
across the sand
he seemed far away
like a gull bracing
the clean salt wind,
he seemed close
like the piece of drift
in my pocket.
Like words said once.
Like what will come.

Alsea Tidewater

There's a basic flat the river gives you here
hills can't disturb. Mooring piles are capped
with gulls. A little path leads up from mud
where each house waits to count the next slack tide.
There is one bridge – kids cross, and smile,
and carry plastic bags. They never need
to say elk walk the road a mile or two
upstream. As if this never changed.
As if cheap wine you get in Waldport casts
an amber glow on findings by the sedge.
Herons can't be moved from what they find.
At five each afternoon the lighthouse light
is checked by keepers who drive out.
Some rocks are dangerous past the mouth.
Remember this from summer: silt
collects below the sand. Never trouble twice
about the way floods bring new wood
and rearrange the berm – the gull
that circles roughly overhead is in control.
You've been down here before the roads were black,
before the last green bridges lost their paint.
Sun on your left, you guess it's time to turn
back to the road that takes you to your source.
Just passing through, you understand.
The way the light runs up, the way the river
yawns and turns to rest before the sea.

North of Likely

I came this way to taste some empty
fields, stroked yellow stubble
framed in rust wire and horizon.
At GAS and EAT I came to stop.
No combine or coyote walked the wheat.
The salty shape below rimrock
was shadow, hope of hawk, a yellow line
down 95 long as my longing.
A low line of mountains, distant, deep cyan,
was full of cats. Silence was never
this full. A chromed Olds coasted in on empty,
stopped wanting even one thing more
than this. I came this way
to stand in air, which is to say
I didn't talk about the color of maps.
Full of dollar gasoline and Crush
I came to know the light
dry wind would catch the falling paint.

In the Last Oak Meadows

The *Large Marble* is extinct, unknown
why, probably fed on wild mustard.
Thirteen specimens are held
around the world: last taken, 1908.

The *Zerene Fritillary* ate violets
as a larva. It can't be found.
It's a name no one can trace.

Propertius Dusky Wings hides in ground debris
over winter. They're raked
and bagged, they're burned
with trash from urban forests.

Moss's Elfin lives with rocks.
The *Ringlet* prefers grass.
Where we see such empty space
we build.

The *Common Banded Skipper* – but try
to find one.

The last meadows are fenced.
The ministry would like to spray, and will,
and will we know
when iridescent wings,
quiet as the oaks,
are gone?

Look close by lupines –
Icaroides Blue is possible.
They say one lives
in a recent clearcut near Shawnigan.

Postcard from Vermilion Cliffs

Above the fabled canyon
camcorders pan the view.

Promises rim the gorge:
Red penstemon, dead pine.

I can't get past the beauty
I'm supposed to see.

Pink hoodoos, weathered
limestone, lie exposed –

the limits of my language.
A raven drops into

the space I overlooked.
At home I'll play it back

and in that false light
I'll tell you what it means.

1st Avenue South

where weeds do well
between warehouses
in sidewalk cracks
        plaintain
        foxtail
        wirestemmed daisies
even, by a chainlink fence,
        horsetail and blackberry

where all love exposure, disturbed
                ground
        where
is the ground?
only cement

where a man sleeps in a colorless flower

        find him

Letter from Saanich

B: already a full season since the meeting
in the mountains. We writers with some concept
of the wild (concept-less) stood on a real
batholith with words. Do you still get out
to breathe immensity & minutiae in some
swirling system? in the fractals of chaos landscape
chant? Here, more flickers & jays than I've seen
in the burbs do their thrash & swoop, even
cougars (some say green-eyes glow) around the park
& schoolyard lands. We (the writers' hands)
go out & we (of night and north) come close,
always meet where we are. My window view a cedar
hedge, an empty plum, horizon canopy of oak,
few roofs, part of a fence & lots of sky & cloud –
that changing light & hue frames the minutes.
I could go down on my face through the surface
leaves into the anarchy of early winter, but
you are probably already there. In *The Globe and Mail*
I read that polar bears near Churchill suffer
in the warming trend – less body fat, shortened
bay-ice season for floe-hunting, & snowy owls
can find no snowshoe hares or lemmings, die
flying south. The convergent spike of climate
& plunge of populations, wild or otherwise,
disaster for this year's cubs & fledglings. One friend
busies himself vituperating philological critique,
you know, what is art; another is trying to finish
two-years' work on her novel, has come from snowy

mountain seeking city-lights intensity to fuel
the final rush her characters demand. We promise
we will keep in touch. With the lid blowing off
these very inner worlds I see a hermit thrush, pumps
thin leg, picks invisible insects from the leafy lawn
in agitated intervals. We do work on, find our song.
Send me a section of that. Love, G.

From Bright Angel Point

If I had an expeditionary allotment
:like John Wesley Powell
:like Lewis and Clark
:like Darwin, Huxley, Haeckel
to learn the lay of the land
:the #'d h.ways
:the scenic b.ways
:everything else in the way of ways
I w'd catch it all, rolling along

then: in next life
sit
and draw the flowers

sit with pencil
in hand
by the strange
beauty
orange globemallow
&
white
evening
primrose
& listen

Writing This

1

here is no   not any thing comes
so   any way   push the empty
like   dog's head out car window
50 mph   grin   tongue hangs
nose to wind   everything
just   to   move
across the paper   when there
is nothing to say   write that way

2

what does that do   what
does that do   to go on
in it   days ago
when back   there
came to that   meaning
well   it was   done
somehow   what any
thought they did   could
do what was   meant
how going on   does that

3

right this not the or any middle
unless   at one extreme is
you point it   to me   is an
edge sort of like   a drop off
where any way you   where I could
if it was a want   to start some
this   kind of thing is what   do
on each field white   a ritual
make me see the   go on   it
is like   falling   I did
in dream now do   for me I
keep at this   for it is that
so real to always   again it
nothing else   know what   is
scratching   like behind a wall
right for seeing what   I write

4

with what   is in mind   it's
wow   I'd like to write that down
                                   a break in that
a nod   could follow   lead   give
pull   push   over
a rough spot   fallen tree
wash out   fell asleep   could
go right along   no break
in that   track a dream   into
what   day   a thought through
forgetting   there is nothing
outside of that   everything
contour   movement   vibrating
I touch   in what   touches

5

I feel is moving all what don't
I know is hitting the water
hard a kingfisher wake
cold what is in my mouth

Foxglove Time

how to look, not
knowing how to begin

a bunch of petal-tubes
at the base

swollen ovaries
drying, filling

galaxies inside worlds
bumblebees know

at the growing tip
the green promise

beyond that, sky,
no end in sight

how to see, not
knowing how to end

2

quartz to quartz

: but to test the center
you have to go all the way both ways:

A.R. Ammons,
Sphere: The Form of a Motion

Downed Pine on Shell Beach

Drab willets on the mud flash black and white
bold wings. One gull
and more than twenty rested cormorants

jump off a float and splash,
lift, fly in six directions, skim
the sleeping Thursday bay.

On quartz and orange feldspar granite sand
bruised clumps of stonecrop
lie by bundled needles where bole and crown

of a fallen Bishop pine,
with spiny cones enclosed by bark and wood
attached, has crashed.

Strange to see it from
this point of view. Look up – an empty nest
is close. The roots are sky.

Wild Radish

It's grown beyond reason
between the two lanes
and the thistly bull pasture,
a fence-high tangle rank
with pastel four-winged
flower heads, tough greens
and still wet snap pods.

It's a lesson in edges,
the roughness of form. Count
petals, opercula, guess
where the first one first
set root, set shape. Set
to page the way the eye
makes what it sees in it.

It's not alone; not
the only plant to fill
the niche of fullness,
beauty consummate:
syllables of light
following the last days
of nothing, nothing.

It's a cross-shaped flash
seen close, before it fruits,
beaked, clinging
season-long. It's

the sound in the name
for the image in the thing.
Raphanus; radish.

It's found with hemlock,
bird's foot, flax.
Maybe crossed with
charlock in the old world,
maybe not. The pasture
grazed, field mowed,
road molten and trod –

it's breaking these plains
of culture, in strips
left fallow. Knit tangle
waist-high, knot of weed
words brink and peer
to follow. Now goldfinch,
now the whole kingdom.

Like Rain or Snow

Not out of any dream
the parachutist appeared
over the valley –
the Rogue River country empty
but for oaks and grasses burnt,
or dead, we couldn't decide –
a speck hatched from a Cessna.
We marveled at that,
said no, no way, count me
out. Not brief moments
of freedom like that,
daring happiness to end
or try us one more time.
Climbing the mountain
road south of Ashland
you touched my leg, you held
my eyes. I saw the sky then,
saw it held us, collecting
pieces of water and ice
before letting them find
their own way down.

Flash Flood

The creek rose over the top today.
Risen tires left tracks on silt.
Half a block upstream, upstreet, a fence
gave way, the wire pulled from post
by the rush. A piece of pepperwood
unwrapped itself from history.
Shed bark confettied on the surface.
With a grace we thought was easy
the living snapped; the storm made clear
no other way. Knee deep clipping
brush to help the flow I felt the tug below.
A red unlike madrone was woven there.
A spotted skink held tight as I to wood,
never knowing it would never be the same.

Heads

after a triptych by Dennis Brown

1

Take all three canvasses
as one. A progress
left to right is set
the way we read.
All are heads,
all deal in blues and reds.

2

Bandages. There had been eyes.
This face will never see us.
The one hidden wants
the silence we entertain
between us, first and last.
There is some blood.

3

Until the gesture of a head
from the back. Not knowing
if sight has been restored
we reach a hand
into the green beyond
the wall we face.

4

There still remains
a regular, split
four-sided red and green,
something to do with where

the eyes should be,
lost inside the blue-to-the-edges world.

5

All three seen at last
as separated frames,
negatives in a punched-out universe
where no eyes see us.
The absence of contact
is what keeps us looking.

Picnic

Our skin don't you think is only so thick
and what connects us at times is our enmity.
So much for Pythagoras. Start with
a given: there is a place by the creek
within three walls of hemlock and one
of nothing. Holsteins across the creek
remain as ignorant as we want them
while we pop the cork, slice cheese and open
each our own book to the places we had marked.
"Can I read you something?" I, or you, say,
and blackbirds settle in droves along our edge.

The Other Side

A breeze of balsam and coriander on her lips,
her signature on nervous skin. A net
of plusses seeking minuses, inevitable.
Sand in our shoes, beach love, sweet sherry,
one-gull afternoon, then sleep under skylight
and a dream – the Statue of Liberty dancing
with the Colossus of Rhodes seen from the open
bomb bay of an old Navy transport droning overhead.
This longing above, as below, each for the other side.

Chinese Wish Papers

Cheap vermilion and Hershey's Kisses gold foil
on thin joss paper squares in cellophane
distributed by Wing Man for seventy-nine cents.
The package is opened – did I make a wish from this
set of opportunities, was it the time you and I
drove up Mount Vision in a storm, parked by the side
of the road and lit them, each our secret, against
the wind and the future? Or did I only wish to wish,
making ready for the world of friends, offering
small magic, wanting the world of jays and osprey
to continue to include us? I knew, before you said
watch out, what you wish for may become true,
the responsibility that comes with hope. I knew
you had to stay alive to learn how it all turned out.

Sonnetina

having come by way of losing
to the prospect of being lost
another way of seeing
that sad condition

a hole in the skin
inside
in
                    — sigh

a grand profusion:
no matter
what I do
all I see

is you and you
're not even here

Shaky

Am I in love?
  Panic is no picnic.
  I miss her in bed.
Am I a puppy dog?

I bring her coffee.
  Am I in love?
  Does she find me boring?
I rub her feet.

Does she miss my touch?
  I am lonely and dizzy.
  I call a few times.
Am I in love?

I stay in the room.
  Does she still like to dance?
  Am I in love?
Reading poems to myself.

Am I in love?
  I wait for the mail.
  I walk too slow.
Does she howl at the moon?

I'm afraid we will drift.
  Am I in love?
  Am I finally whole?
I am afraid I will drift.

Does my need repel?
  I imagine her lips.
  I write love on the walls.
Am I in love?

I'm my only condition.
  Am I in love?
  Do I dwell on words?
In the motionless air.

Am I in love?
  I'm a Doric column
  in a temple of love.
A classical myth?

Do I wear a mask?
  Am I in love?
  A terrible mask?
Am I in love?

Liturgy: *Qui erat et qui est*

Tremendum

she, by window

this feeling
                                        see, it
shrinks to fit in a frame
incurring lapse of
vital thought
calling for
simple names, of
self, icons whose
referents are those of
                                        heart, which
mind once
knew as all it needed, not
to understand, to live

then surface minute silences

Credo

faith – if full, be given
the graces necessary

tepid become fervent
mounting to perfect

following novena, the final
penitence – bondage to you

Mysterium

black

receives light and holds it

I have tried to see into it –
your eyes – but I have never

while you smile and talk
worried about dying

and even when I saw

you kiss him – another world
I love that too

for everything lost – is found
in full spectrum white

Lacrimosa

the intent is – go figure
live in a place – still in love
without – but music
fill the cave-in – with smoke
plunge, every time – nothing
breathe – me
get out get out – move
in air – am contained
what anyone says – break
like falling – stars

Dies Irae

last light, choose dark
lead, write big

don't look far for
assonance – one night

hawk roar, off
in tremolo, in the now

that is – to say –
accept that – no

a wind rises then
calm and a wind rises

no never need but now
I tell myself – except what

would have been – is
almost dark enough

to let it go – can't see
too good – blowing away

Night Walk in Inverness

Walk the street under oak canopy under
cloud cover under the vacuum of space
where stars rearrange statically
like cat hairs on a shag carpet.

Trust the feeling in the feet as they
fill the socks and press against
the inner sole against the interface
of pebbled tarmac and the tread.

Listen for the crunch of losing
the unseen way, the edge
where arboreal particles collect
beside the ditch beside the hill.

Notice the dark parked car
you barely noticed in the day,
the '58 Bel Air that never reached
home. Its rust. Its place of rest.

Town Dog

I sneaked downstairs, not that it mattered,
no one was home. I let myself out the door
into the night, freely, being human.
I lay down in the middle of the street,
hands clasped behind my head,
exhaling once, mightily. The trees moved
with breezes they caught from that.
Wanting everything, but quietly,
this slow dance, these maybe kisses.
No one noticed. It was good to talk
with you tonight, then fade as I desired
before the moon rose. Yes, very human.
I slept there in near silence, oblivious
as the dog who walks as good as dead
across Highway One, then stops to scratch.

Letter from Wawona

Dear G: I'm learning birds by sound.
The flicker's *keer,* the nuthatch *bzzz*
fix in my ear. The silences between
catch even more: the empty trees,
the sky, granite boulders fixed
along a dry fall river bed.
Low water, cool and cloudy day,
a few brief spots of rain, a breeze, some sun.
I learn John Muir fell in love hard here,
became lost, walked his range of light
for endless days. And I learn the brilliant blue
mayfly lives only a day with wings
having emerged from the stream without a mouth
which, in feeding, would impede its functional
desire to mate. The shocking scarlet wild
fuchsia's blooming to attract whatever
last insects are driven to intensity.
All iambs tend to sad; spondees cut quick.
Poetry is more than this. Even in the world of rocks
likes attract: quartz to quartz, olivine
in frozen pools of green, the darker shapes
in diorite. Each mineral finds itself.
But I am not yet crystal, pure or hard,
though all things here speak through geology.
I say to myself, *your solitudes*
in not so many syllables – reminding me
of you. Each morning here is new.
I think you'd smile to know
we're not more final than the birds.
Even if no one's here to hear, they sing,
bring everything to heart. Take heart. Love, G.

Sheriff's Call to Platform Bridge

She had worked through the afternoon above the creek,
sandpapering the stone, erasing the old names and dates,
clearing a space and honoring it with a patch of blue.
Holding her pain in her determination, she said his name,
a quiet refrain almost beneath her sharp, short breaths
while she spray-painted her initials and his, which he
would never see. When the deputy arrived, he cited her.
There was no denying the law had been breached again.
For a moment it seemed a truth had reached the other side.
A school of small trout quivered in the green translucent pool.

My Nothing

my saying this
myself saying
it's *a good thing*
yellow rain
nothing but music
a good, good thing
the gash of this
my wanting
my following this into
a betweenness now
of nothing *a good thing*
yellow clouds
nothing but remember
how close, yellow rain
stalled
nothing but no words
between, and of nothing
music more echo
the thing of what it was
where she sat
nothing but a thing
a good thing, yellow
becoming *a good, good thing*
the direction is clear
I want you but
nothing

Impossible

August 31, 1997

You simply attempt
to escape into the world
where no one
notices. You want nothing
but a late-night snack.
At an intersection
a black sedan, a rush of recognition, and
you accelerate into a tunnel
mad with the possibility
of this kind
of birth.

Finding the Phoebe by the Bay

Black-mantled shadow, branch-bound possibility
with eyes of certainty you sit no longer than the moment
we take to take you in, to name, cross-reference, predict
the pattern of the flight you will most likely take for food.
Always by water's edge, always by day, collecting
packages the world has for you, adding, adding
in your parabola mid-rise – no forced geometry there.
Sum and fulfillment, stitchery and bindery of the whole,
out, and out, in a dart and return response to the way
within the eye. You form within your style, *venture and pluck,*
your name which we might never know but see as what you do.
For every one by one discovery, with seconds, years between,
of you, like you, we dance lightly – lucky, incredulous –
home, home being once again our own next leap.

3

a new geometry

As the same fire which makes the soft clay hard makes hard wax soft.

Virgil, *Eclogues*

California

marble bust by Hiram Powers, 1858
(De Young Museum, San Francisco)

is a woman – in her marble eyes – no doubt
no wrap – heaven is on her shoulders
young in the field – yellow hair tied back
her full breasts wait – for a man who
will find nuggets in the mountains
orchards in the valleys – wisps of her gold
and for children – her arms find themselves
holding – water, her lips – watersheds
her cold white smile – the future of the state

Old Napa

for LB

The garden in her front yard has rooted
deep since the horse-hitch days

it was planted in floodplain topsoil
banked behind streetside walls

of cement. The house stands like a fortress
centered in a moat of hydrangea and rose.

The doily trim and shutters, newly painted
faint cerulean, the leaded glass, the cornerstone

of river rock, the vaulted portico –
the main idea and details remain intact.

Some blocks away my aunt lies to be viewed
in state, fall flowers her surround, glasses fixed,

fingers waxed in prayer. Her doors are open
to the street. *Rock of Ages* holds us in the air.

Rekindled

A tracery of red in your white,
a fine net, makes me think at first
you've been crying, even though I know
it's only been a day since they enetered
with lasers and tiny suction pumps
to remove the film between you
and the world. Still, you might be
crying, tears gathered on your lashes
after the storm has passed.
Your face has opened. You tell me
clouds are white again, surprised
the living room wall is lightest blue,
not the yellow dull you had come to
believe. Now there is another chance
the world is large, and I find the blue
in your center I had forgotten. I find
my own eyes clearly reflected there.

South Fork Merced River

After the flood
a new geometry

The old round
granite rolling
too slow for eyes,
a million year project

A hard sugar
pine cone cut by
a chickaree
nearly misses
knocking me out

Mercy!

River egg-rocks
rattle, carving potholes,
carved themselves
by rock-rich water

And all catch light –
Skipper wings,
Sister wings,
Sulfur wings

In this riverbottom where
everything
runs down to
winter, this life

Above, this life
below, this life
found

Elanus

Soon it will be lined with grass
under a riparian sky,
lined with down and the heavenly

couple stretched with good wine
on the foothill, fine cymbals
pounding air to particles of gold

and the vault of God leaking
stubble and moss on
their solitary lovemaking.

They are named *Kite,* their bed
is flimsy, large and deep.
The root of their joy is hovering.

Finding the *Imprimitura*: San Pablo Bay

We enter from the north, quietly parting
knit thistles and tough old spider threads,
the knots that bind the sea-salt level bay.

A subtle cooling, low and layered, loosens
the palsied smoky quota.
Enough: now we will seek the ground.

Tules suggest sinkholes hidden in the marsh.
Choosing again, we breach the ancient
bramble fence and stand square on the datum

holding ocherous pappus darts in hand,
next to nothing, minding this moot mora.
Before the light is lost, fine inspiration

en plein air. With the rising of vespers
the canvas, nearly sleeping,
softens even further toward dun.

The Event

after Richard Misrach, The Desert Cantos

Some of us are here to watch, most
of us are here to watch for what to
watch. We have camped out on
the cracked saline earth in a row
along the line they set for us.
Comfort stations are available
on the horizon. It will be history.
There is a lot of waiting. There is time
to polish the shell of the Airstream,
the Winnebago, the Cherokee.
Look at all the empty folding chairs.
Too hot to sit still, not knowing
when it will happen. We have brought
coolers and drinks, we are prepared.
We have plenty of beer, and we
expect the landing to be memorable.
If everything goes as expected,
it should happen soon.

At the Ropes Course

for AH

My eyes were drawn to the high risks,
the log cross, tree climb, leap of faith,
but yours, not only due to fear of height
were drawn to things much closer –
cat tracks in wet sand, gold frogs,
slug and millipede, salamander
by the creek – such things seen are true.
At dusk, "Look, Greg, a bat. Another one."
Satellites nearly too faint to find, and mars.
"Look at that star – it's spinning –
now it's getting farther away."

Instant knowledge. Ownership of the instantly
seen, soon gone. And later, trusting the belay
fourteen feet above the ground you saw
mosaic with pink rocks and orange-red lilies,
your hands on solid staples in the tree
let go to drift connected down
in that illuminated world
where motes of light called butterflies
become the ordinary miracles of sight.

His Gloves

From their soft red interior, a warm smell
of gasoline, kerosene, twenty-weight crude
and red alder creosote of trees felled by chain
held to boles two feet up by hands that came
to work. Hands that slowly slid into
the hardened sheaths, into the history
of dangerous things: brambles dared,
dogs' teeth bared against their will.
Safe and wild, able and strong,
fingers curling into purposes within,
thumbs opposing flat necessities.
Limits were stretched to meet the job
yet they remained the same good fit
for years. Empty, unused on the workbench
now he trembles, they remain
as gestures embracing his own.

Postcard from Harney County

Driving the same road the same road
until a sprinkle of blackbirds

as if seen from the egg looking up at the sun
a paragraph of commas, essay of ellipses,
minutes and hours and seconds come loose

punctuating nothing

cross the road
and their shadows cross
the road.

Cholona Siding, Nevada

It's a long drive, but all students of human folly should do it.
P. Reyner Banham, *Scenes of America Deserta*

In the glossy four-by-six
artifact of summer
rails slice through alkali,
iron laid on salt – converge

at nothing, sky. The desert
is not diminished by roads. God,
a hawk perched on a pole,
a row of fence appears in white.

Heat bends the far range.
I take the picture,
pick and bind
the sage with string below

the crushed rock grade. Silence,
a raven, nothing – a kind of nothing
circles the horizon
beyond the unseen edge.

Fort Rock Desert

six miles out to spatter cone
vermilion paintbrush brittle juniper
firkin beer dry rot sheds
yellowjacket fire ring
six calibers of shells strewn round
wilderness study site
fine flower sage sun low moon low
as far as the Jeep and I could go
red ants black sand dull flies
wind rush sweet grass

Yes, it had
something to do with you.

Smoke Creek to Sulphur

Nothing, Nevada, where minerals
give names to mountain blocks risen
above the cracks in the sand
and cobble playa, the rippleless bajada,
the riches there mostly imagined.
Black Diamond deep in the Fox Range,
Selenite at empty Empire. Dry, dead horse
washes follow alluvium below Lear Peak.
At the wan expanse of Ascalon
no roads, but twin track traces, gate after gate
all open. Black Rock landmark
floating north against the Calicoes.
Placerite, abandoned mine. Cinnabar,
the tailings fenced. A windmill
rusted dry near Bill DeLong's Well.
At the edge of the map, Last Chance
before the Winnemucca run.

Mammoth Mountain

for BY

finding this as language incarnate

(before significance consummates
infinitely seriatim)

what is not and what is
here – silica rockedge, lapilli pumice,
horned lark tinkling (walks, does not hop)

          little black water bugs in seething spring
(bite! patiently waiting)

black scat twist on the summit

Homeless

A few steps from the street
a double door, closed,
no knob, no latch,

panels made to swing
from within. In its way
a white shroud

solid as a keel
is, as wall is, found
as part of a design.

Beneath, the story
in the stained near-comic
bas-relief, the form

the prostrate symbol
cover cloth conceals
sleeping

in the world
where animals
cogitate and nod.

Partisanship

I keep misreading
"vote" as "wolf."
Modern white versals
against blue federal ink
in my midrange ocular
scan of election year
floor junk mail
bring me at least twice
to a near full stop.

It must have to do with
an aesthetic occupation.

Soon I will no longer be
able to stay within the lines
I drew to build upon to dance.

My candidate will start to howl.
I will drop pretense and choose
the greater of two goods.

When I run no one will lose.

The Commonplace

for DMD

This taking paper and pen, sitting to write. Briefly
touching the familiar in the new air
of each breath: the intense present: flickers,
a dyad of quiet voices, yesterday's rain become a sidewalk stain,
a bunch of sweet white grapes shrinking on a red-leafed vine.

The world goes on, quieter, as if a part of it were removed.
        More quietly.
We move around within the house as if learning to dance.
In the slow river a turtle rises to nick the surface for air.
        No ripple.
Something bright – an egret, an agate – faded, yet
still whole in mind, as ground glass conceivably holds
        particulars.

My mother heard herself outside. She reached for something
        we couldn't see.
The ceiling in her room was an open window. She knew I knew
she knew. The sounds of our voices held us there, but now
the present tense takes hold. October. A few more minutes.
        Leaves.

Dogtown Morning Glory

Three years, five years later, no sign
of those floods remain, but blackbirds
and flies, warblers and sapsuckers,
and the sky closed and the air kept
by nettles and thistles pressing in
and rampant brambles taking over
an abandonment, windows broken, doors sprung.
Once rich hues now jaundiced and rouged
and where the roadside radish hedge is cut
white-on-white butterflies, a rank mix
of plant sex and decay, willow balsam
and poison hemlock breaking through
the dark romantic tapestry (as the sun
the clouds). A redwing multitude rises
from some invisibility of marsh and almost
everything finally begins to move.

4

the acquistorium

Observe, random energist,
the bear's placidity.

Theodore Roethke,
Straw for the Fire:
From the Notebooks, 1943-63

First River Watch

In the language of light an epistle
of subtle reminders, and from those,
adjustments – in seeing, as if seen by

the weather (beyond the restraint
of the idea of weather), the tides
offering imminence and release

twice daily, the changing boundaries
of the visible on the opaque
jigsaw pieces of the surface where

rain drops arrive as if from below
with momentum to break through, leaping
free of it and free to return.

Lit in a dark field, occasions –
in some, a shadow, in some the core
of a shadow, making a mirror of,

questioning the movements of
those who look in, into, almost through,
and of those who might be found there.

Desideratum: Red Feather

for CP, at Five Brooks

opaque carnelian crystal held
          no red feather on the hand
xanthin in the drying veins
          no red feather on the leaf
great blue rests in willow scrub
          no red feather on the branch
dehiscent *Rubus* petals catch
          no red feather on the vine
cardinal scarlet tanager
          no red feather on the east
aphrodite, swallowtail
          no red feather on the path
tangle of grey down teased out
          no red feather on the kill
turkey vulture soars aloof
          no red feather on the sky
green duckweed late spring algae scum
          no red feather on the pond
grunt and bullfrog splash is gone
          no red feather on the sound
blue darner, sanguine butterfly
          no red feather on the sun
blushing secret picnickers
          no red feather on the kiss

no red feather on the ground
my eyes were open all the way
but now, above – sweet *konk-la-ree* –
          red feather on the wing

Grebe

per -
fectly
in place in
control
float - or sink -
ing not not
not thinking

all sur -
face
a matter of
density
with -
in that
pur -
pose never
art as art -
i -
fice

one eye
out one
in

always be -
come all
ways one
ever -
y thing is

and looks and
sees and
there you have it

dives

Argumentum Odonatum

> *The dense and moist and cold and dark came together here…*
> *and the rare and hot and dry went out to the farthest part of*
> *aether.* Anaxagoras of Clazomenae

From the water at night
we naiads
emerge and cling
to the solid and rest
and wait for light.

We instars
embody change.
Mandibles reform.
Thorax splits.

We tenerals
pull ourselves out
of the exuvium.
Legs and wings
unfold and harden.

Wings!

We darners, skimmers,
emeralds, and bluets
have come this far
from the river bottom
knowing no other way.

Now, with a thousand ways
to see
we leave the drying molt behind
for air.

Energy and Matter at South Jetty

where you draw the line broken *Spisula* shells
reform as
frail and bright crescents

if one should fall right there
light in there coming out
the seeds of the tide

seen as imperfect, entered as such mineral seaworn
edges erode
passing illumination

a sense of small completions,
common findings
arising and passing away
in the the sign of the constant

flux itself may be a thing
a fluid context
as each solid drift is picked
a story

apprehended, chosen a tale of redemption
plucked whole from the ground
gesturing in the radiance

Little Bend in the River Song

From the deck
the high tide line
is visible on
the dry green shorebank
grass and sedge

where every
thing
which seems
still moves.

A door is open to the sun
to the nearly soundless
cormorants, grebes,
to the fully silent
horsetail, skunk cabbage,

an opening in the light
into the sound of under
every flying, leaping
diving, dabbling, whole and edgy,
swimming, rooted,
touching, breaking through,
above, below all

surface.

Letter from Clatsop

To find one thing-sized word with which to start to catch
the time since last I wrote, some sentential form to say
the thing beyond hello. Dear J, a cold front sudden wind
around the hill from the west this hour pulls the house and
chains against the boom, then back, swings us out and back
enough for vertigo, breaks tension of the brackish water
in long sinewed ladders of reflected light. This calls rain, it
hits the roof tin hard again, we hear the little rivers run
from land and splash into the lower river, here where low is
twelve feet vertical from high – large worldview, then small,
widening circles uncircling in their near contemporaneity, rain
nodding its identity with river: So elemental causation
deconstructs the ideal. Pythagoras passed through one day,
shook out his umbrella, moved on. This morning, tomorrow,
a grebe the first on scene at dawn seems not to notice though
we guess she does. Buddha-calm, with feathers in her gut, slow,
she sinks by willing it, submerges without diving – or with.
Would we learned our own weight in water, let alone in air and land,
could change like that and does like weather. Happily, having
found some few but strong words in this wet northwest
floating edge-becoming-center-coming-edge of present minutes,
surfacing to write and send them your way as the cormorant
rises from deep with fish, swallows, shakes it down, and runs
upstream to fly to god-of-the-cormorants knows where, I am
waiting only for what comes, in ebb and flow, this way. This
is what comes. This way the paradox of how to start is but
an echo of impossibility. I would love for you to hear a chorus
and verse of this new impressive life. Come sit on the deck,
the dock, by the window and see. Love, G.

Seven Transparencies

Cathlamet Bay, Columbia River

1

the longer I stand at this edge where the sky is
road and river, the more immense is the world
into which you become smaller (than the trees,
than their dark reflections, than thinking)

2

more clear, the impenetrable scumble
of the opposite shore is released from Earth
and where the wind has begun to texture
the image, no sign of your wake remains

3

nothing but the slightest trace of a wash of blue

4

nothing at all

5

and the eye brought low lights
the minute precisely, now
are forms of grey on grey more
(*formal* comes to mind) formed

6

and later, less lit from behind and none
from the sky, where sepias are nothing
but fading sepias – you have to touch
the surface of things like this to see –

7

I have this dream where a river overflows
and changes course, in the dark and private
confine of a winter night, and in the morning
I touch the untouched sand it left behind

Vespers: Starlings in Astoria

Each is singular, each a particle
of a whole, pausing briefly as one
then resuming as the ten thousand

coming together in themselves
reflected in the jewel facets
of a net, restlessly drawing in

before the roost, below the river sky,
lit by lasts of sun. Each finding each
they become one and drop, heavy,

below the Ninth Street pier.

A Painter's View

Lower Columbia River Estuary

It began then by its currentside, that first
translucent pearl blue running under graphite
indigo strata which had become fused and
now were separating, but not quickly,
and so the image of a ceiling in a room
which would with trust in opening
dissolve. Then from the west the floor
in turn took in its alabaster and set out
a matte of steel, still blue. Both dimensions
spread and in the rift appeared
the far land, near umber by the edge,
near sepia beyond, the farthest plane gunmetal.
As in certain luminous arts, lights from behind
the veil became articulate – crepuscular rays
with auras of gamboge, haloes, parhelia,
tangent *arcs-en-ciel* displaying slight
intensities of chrome – an intimate assemblage.
In that unmeasured time long-held philosophies
flew, as did five cormorants, fast and low
somewhere far to the east above the river
before its fading twilight moment of cobalt.

Aria – Heart Music
for MJD

These are troubling sounds – some
after doubtful pauses double –

a diastolic drum.
There is no common meter here.

The room is sterile, dimly lit.
Percussive notes of the heart

and distal points of pulse are found
and fixed, the waves' parameters

visualized. And we listen –
I from the chair by the window,

you from the bed – inhabiting the space
between, somewhat closer

when nothing else is necessary.
In this strange new music

the next and the next cardinal beats
are obbligato, minimal, definitive.

Then the cadence declares
the beginning of the song.

The Aquarius Superstructure (Postcard from Reno)

1998 / 1918

Lumps in the soup of matter and energy among which
Your birthday slipped by, I was not looking,
evidence for supergalactic clusters strung together
while every day, up here, has wings, and cloudbursts
like pearls, within which hundreds and thousands
of lightnings; regards to your folks and the valley.
within each of which shine millions of stars.

The Steamer *Casca* Encounters Heavy Ice Enroute to Whitehorse

for HAD

The folds and tears, the faded margins
tell its transit over ninety-three years.
The fixer used was strong: near willow buds
are textured still, the snow on cordwood
on the deck is near pure white, while
the smokestack, far shore spruce, all things
around the people hatted and akimbo on the bridge
remain near black. The boat is held by two lines
to the nearly frozen Yukon's edge. He must have
jumped the six feet to the shore with tripod,
box, and hood, and framed with his quick eye
and shot. What they were then; what he was there.
Signed in the corner in cursive bleach.
I read his risky joy in this cold silver print
and in his later penny postcards of delight.

Night Poem

While she slept, outside
the inner logic of dreams
particles of comet dust
flared brief arcs
from the virtual pattern of stars
called The Lyre.
As they inscribed their questions
for Earth, Earth answered
from the mouths of its babies,
wailing and yipping back in the hills,
intense and short-lived as meteors.
When all this had passed
she woke and faced the open window
where the moon
was framed, blue and cold,
and lay awake for awhile
in the greater silence
breathing the planet's breath.

Lonchaeid Fly

Clinging to the jewel case
liner notes of Penderecki's
Fluorescences for orchestra
the shiny black
big oval-eyed plant-eater
languishes in the glare
of the sixty watt bulb
of the gooseneck lamp
in the plantless room
where I sit up late and write.
Flops, legs up, recovers
and crawls between
the rollers of the printer
and back out and flies
and lands again there.
A buzzing *akin to chaos;*
this animal is misplaced.
What to do. Cling
to the modernist maxim,
the present predicament
presented in all possible
ways, until resolution,
as in the apex, to a pure *C,*
before falling apart again.
And to what the light offers.

Ultima Ratio Regum

on announcement of intention to attack

Little medusa, what do you have to do
with the killing brought on by killing?

You are free swimming, little more
than floating in your own necessity,

unknown as any fauna overlooked
in a complex system, by a higher order,

until stirred from your place in the warm mud
waters by my warm cupped hand.

And what have the ubiquitous sea slug,
the gunnel and ghost shrimp,

the heart cockle and the spiny sculpin
to fear in that same sustaining medium,

that ritornello of days and years
on the saltings of the Skagit Sea?

A periodic question, ending with a period.
For today we have heard *the final argument of kings.*

Honoring the deeper tradition,
I set you back into the slack tide

with a petition: *Mend this broken world.*

Nahcotta Tidelands

Picture this – an idiom,
an image seen (worth
x number words), a way
to capture splinters
of light and form, is found.

Forget the state I'm in – mind
is made of and for these pale
ochres and deep indigoes
of hills, the unframed
sky, the intervening bay.

The foreground green golds
argue against narrative.
Certain particulars stand in for
royalty: sheaths of marsh
grass in the field of great heron.

Neither start nor end –
eyes newly open
at this edge, this line, this
vanishing point. Somewhere
behind me, crows comment
from another point of view.

First Record of *Field Crescent* in Gray's Harbor County

Obtaining but our own extent / In whatsoever Realm
Emily Dickinson

This tawny nymphalid
was overlooked before

It was overlooked by us.
Until we'd seen, and seen

Again, our eyes
drawn over fore and hind,

Dorsal, ventral, noting
slight and subtle shadings

Indicating *P.pulchellus.*
Drawing close to verify,

On the south side
western mountain

Avalanche meadow
yellow summer stage,

In the dazzling, flitty, flighty
show of the insect myriai

We found this single, small, one,
this one in question,

And now consider
its momentary aspects,

its dark and orange presence
further proof of the real.

5

knot

No specific finitude is an ultimate shackle upon the universe.

Alfred North Whitehead,
Modes of Thought

Inventum

To untangle a snarl, loosen all jams or knots and open a hole through the mass at the point where the longest end leaves the snarl. Then proceed to roll or wind the end out through the center exactly as a stocking is rolled. Keep the snarl open and loose at all times and do not pull on the end; permit it to unfold itself.
The Ashley Book of Knots

Finding myself, you say, *here,*
is a shock! Once was an end of
all, and now you say, *I know*
now will a beginning be. Thus
our findings in the world-time
of within and of without and
as before and so after remain
thus. Were you not here now
to say *here*, there'd be no knot.

Principium

Sir Isaac Newton, *Proposition VII, Theorem VII*

That there is a power. That there is a basis of mind,
a prime factor, a standard of measure
outside compliance and conformity, as in choice
of these words, as in a lively bravura extended aria
around the insistent complexities of thought. Proof
of how different things are alike. Proof of the structure
of gravity, binding what is to what is, underlying,
overarching, and upon which are founded the phenomena
that accompany phenomena. Evidence of the real
as a newer testament, an empire of sense and number
tending to all bodies at least or at most in part
from an early tongue. That *proportional to the several*
vague universals, is the quality of a particular.
Oh, and of the *quantities of matter.*
There are more than few. And unbelief. And self.
How far can I think about reality [reality . . .]
walking these lines, enumerating, examining,
opening and closing regions of what is,
seeking that *which they contain.*

Hermes and Sol

> *Because each planet corresponded to a metal…an amalgam of the metals would bring the universe into the laboratory. It would be a model of perfect balance between opposites.*
>
> Richard Elkins, *What Painting Is*

Though swift and near my father the sun
I stand here by the vessel of the road
a wooden Mercury, sublimate of coarse red ore
subtile and solitary, an inconclusive presence
visible within three degrees of the moon
by morning calculations, eclipsed by night
and drowned all day in momentary light –
ascending declension, surface oscillation,
curtain to change, cord to rip, truth to tell,
testing the center by extremes –
in questions of faith difficult – diverse,
eloquent, adaptable – a Mercury of brass
amalgamating, stealing and keeping,
rapidly transiting the space inscribed
by this nuclear attraction and genesis
near this brilliant heart of an ancient love,
around and around the core attraction –
the burning recognition in our eyes.

Descriptus

As seen, the form
elaborate, extenuate,

comes from a wound
system, configuring

itself as replica, in that
as within so without.

Hence such as *Volvox,*
green, inhiscent,

involvulated knot
full only of itself

knitting and knitting
till its parts are whole,

its life at any single point
tangential to the set of points

described, inscribed in it
until in spring it springs

and breaks itself into
what only, always, can be.

Passerine

Clock-reckoned time
settles into form,
passes in order
to be, be passing, come.

We think to know, if
not to have or keep
as weight in hand,
timely light. This

morning such a sign –
chickadee at feeder,
sun on spruce,
composed. This then

one passion, the eye
sees through the clock
to the still within.
No bone of previous,

no shell of next.
Its own accompaniment
it spins, existence
tangible, pointing.

Single Barb

Oh – that such can become
in the world as is

found as part of a whole
divided by itself

and isolated as this one
as anything (except zero)

can be (nothing is
a function of never)

as this devilish invention
cut and bent hot

two and a half turns around a wire,
snag, jag, notch,

boundary defining risk
placed there as intention

to keep in, keep out,
left to acquire the rusty patina

of apparent neglect, phenomenally
marginal as these wrought words!

red pear

red pear – the religious aspects – incomprehensible
until a boundary is breached – only beauty
sex – is like a passport – wait for validation – juice
a veritable sea – psychology – a number to count on
invention of reverse – before looking – glass eye
such grapes as fall – in fall – or berries left there
enables – the crossing over, from, into – bibliography
subject – skin – special government vellum
permit – tracery – seal of sensory – irreferential
of a kind – invitation – lunch dance – look it up
with full intention – ferrous indignation – oh desire
there I said it – abstractually – if I am accepted
how the it becomes – particular – expressed
with various endings – the language – register–
on the way a way – kiss – a specific gravity
for each and finally – what to do with feet
that close – and rising and opening and
not by brain – already full – mouth reaches
the sanctorum – say howdy – not one – they
are agreement – so it flows – the two no one
are by fruit – all – mostly taboo – is known

Fleur

How do you first approach
and meet; what do you say?
What books do you carry?
Do you defer or advance,
and when, and how much?
What to note, denote,
annotate, attach, whether to
pick and press, and what to
leave in exchange? How to
perceive and assess the impact
of the field of color, the
wholeness of the organism,
the fullness of the parts,
anther, stigma, corolla, root,
the family ties, ancestry and
inheritance? Where does the
individual begin and where
end? How do you feel about
what you see, and does she
respond in kind? Do you
perceive this as opportunity?

this caught
interleaf
and adjusted
slightly to dry
pigmented cellulose
between two
pressing
sides
of the same
argument
moved to stasis
implying,
allowing,
identification
at one's leisure
by inspection
of the relative
measurements
within a general
agreement
of recognition:
Tiarella

On the Elements

With gods and lesser beings, shakers
of the basic, unchangeable state
of substance, pure and drawn from ore
of Earth, sublimate, condensate,
precipitate of the starting place

giving rise to forms in all the spheres
of air, water, rock, ice, and the excited
states of the living – neutral or charged
nominal energies, the macrocosm
on both sides of orbit and shell,

trope and isotope, placer and crust,
rudiments of qualitative nature
spinning, vibrating, caught in near-
unfathomable eddies and webs
of chaos born and pregnant – bearing

promises and deceit, that this is and is
and this is permanent – even as
burning reveals reductive ash,
as particles are lost and gained,
as ferric yields to ferrous in the ultimate

core, the incipit core, the crucible,
the severest test of calcination
at the heart, in the heart of every
material instance – we take the host
trillions of times until we too dissolve.

Composition

Olivier Messiaen, *Quatuor pour la fin du temps*

enclosed	Having once, and many times again
in medallions and trefoils	as if for the first time, beheld the stained gla
	windows of Chartres and St. Chapelle
	he received his catechism, and the filtered
	refractions fell like benediction
green spirals,	around his eyes and his ears. Listening
which move and turn	to that Gloria, absorbing its spectrum
with the sounds	he said he saw what anyone could see
	in such dazzling music – its chords
diffusing to white rising	of sixteen-tones, its strokes of praise
a prelude	to God and Christ, its tangle of rainbows –
to the unspeakable	and for its duration, the opportunities to he
and the invisible	brilliant intimations of a radical light.

Gift of the Grand Gesture

after Enso (Zen Circle) by Eun (1598–1679),
184th abbot of Daitokuji Temple

This recurrent feeling following having lost,
like a space for a window knocked out of a wall
left empty, like a wall where a window was blown away

is setting for circumscription, for the finest
visible line around minor injuries and sad phenomena:
the chocolate chip batter spilled on the floor.

This line created by, defined by, approaching and touching
both field and form in the void of the paper,
like a flash flood in the desert on a summer afternoon,

has left the space barely changed, somewhat less perfect
and stained with rough ink, like a sign written hastily
by the one who, after all, long gone now, is long gone.

Netsuke

Shape of a rock
carried in my pocket
– lopsided heart – hard
chert
picked up on the Stilliguamish

washed down from some terrain.
We found
each other, lost each other,
again
and again.
It is nothing. Is solid
long as held. Is enough –
these lapses –
and for all intents and purposes –
forever.

Nothing changes
everything.

Westport Compass Rose

At or from
the given or found
center

a string,
a shell,
marks in the sand,

shadows,
cause of shadows,
cessation of shadows.

Know where you are by relationship,
see the seer as if by being seen.

Travel with both compasses, the arc and the pole,
never far from the source of light.

Place becomes text becomes place,
scripted, inscribed, circumscribed.

Drawing the frame, filling it in,
opening it, releasing – beauty –

you can't plan entirely for that.

Homewood

photograph, Lake Tahoe, 1950

coldest,
and sweet pine
still as sound
of waves

•

language I had not learned

•

which I use now having

•

solid folding
chair, sinking
a few inches in granite
sand

•

from street play
from dark held by light in dark room
from sea level home

•

his hat way too big
the horizon perfect
on me, around me

•

circles, I now see

•

said, "Look,"
to me, I thought
to her, knowing
where I was

•

of waves
sand
•
it will never change
I never asked that
it ever, forever
•
such a shadow
I accept
•
was "I am happy"
bound
inside a ring of stone
six thousand feet
and in
finite sky
•
no one has died
language is "I want I am"
enough
•
no not, now
•
when I was
looking in your eye
which blinked
•
feet in the deepest lake
sitting there at the edge

Karbala

Dirt plain.   Scratching, digging in
dodging bullets behind steel rails
by a dead road.   Liberation, dread

as in ratchets burning close to earth
hand-held   potent more as spike than shield.
Sheer force have we   nearing identity

of occupation   control and random abandon
knowing not why   the rainbows of it all
stifling in the suit.   Come quickly salvo

in the desert   heat waves shimmering.
By code name condemned
an honest urge to run for it   jump ditch

become blip of interest.   Moving now from
suddenly nameless   with lost birds   crouching.

First Month, Fifteenth Day

On my dead brother's sixty-eighth birthday, I drive my father through saturated thalo-green and viridian cedar and spruce to Netul Landing, the Lewis and Clark River high and dark from recent rains and runoff. Buffleheads work to stay in place by old, disused pilings.

> An origin, a quest for art; changes towards some end.
> A champion of lost causes, the search to find a friend,
> Then memories of the way back home again.

Farther west, past a field where elk often graze, black cattle feed on hay in a long line across the hill. At Del Rey Beach, storm debris is heaped along the dunes – yard-thick skeins of kelp, driftwood and plastic from the high tide floods along the coast. Near the wrack line we stop, facing the immensity. He says, "It seems smaller." He mistakes a gull on the sand for a ship at sea.

> Kite without wind, string or tail,
> A wing on the sand mistaken for a sail.

Through the open windows we feel cold wet air from the north, the direction the bar pilot's body traveled until it touched land near Copalis, a week ago. He is not that pilot. His white hairs move slightly in that wind.

> Floating, he never found a tether, he was never found
> Until the two worlds met, and he was ground.

He says nothing in or to the loud surf. There seems to be a rare and general agreement.

Reading Room

material at hand, and light.
a recurring shadow outside.

big shaking windows. curtains
of rock crystal, microscopic diamonds.

such immensities block
a whole section of the universe.

choice of nothing. ellipsis in place
of what not. but now

the mystery remains,
codex and stylus

in the vacuumic room.
out, and back. a lit branch,

see it jerk. something moves it
until time. but all night

is long here. variorum.
penultimate. almost enough.

translation: close to disconnect
but pause for something, like thought.

I need not look back into the record of my days or of the geological or any other strata for evidence or proof of the possibility of my existence. Waking before dawn, in the west side morning extension of dream, with the sounds of heron and otter like an emblem on my shield, with a stick of graphite and a sheaf, the window records itself with what words find me then. Chosen, I feel I am and assert. With the written becoming as if to build in place, I find myself in the limited. As any empty space bounded by its own parameters imposed on the existing universe covers or conceals, in the aftermath another is revealed, or all is lost.

Who in Me

knows no beginning –
no, be better than this –

no begotten son forgotten
as is not this, neither this,

nor pun, nor sun or son of son
I ask in the midst of acceleration

be but momentarily foregone
for the motion of. Listens

less for lesson than lingo,
leans for and to the one

who, like me, in fact likes me,
begins to nay-say no. Good, I

can in new self-appreciation
get the gift of gab and go.

By the Old Pier

– the nerves are lit but the page seems small, soft,

porous, flammable, inflammable! compromised,

a question of closed flowers, a black barge of what –

a concept of false or real buttercups –

the walls of the other side of town, collapsing

docks, dependent on weather and certain inconstants,

a wake and the sound of a wake, successive

periods in which time is noted as such and indexed,

some seed pods empty, long boats and artifacts

attached to this or that, still in the wind

– in such a collection

more than I – my eye! – can keep forever,

pieces of matter – some warm, some visibly lit,

scattered finitely, indefinitely – open, openly –

July 5 afternoon sun by the cannery
Sixth Street Pier, sitting
on the tracks facing the river over the edge of

cinder and weeds, stopped with
a cup of hot drink in hand –

seen as it is, as what
could be made of what would have been

seen as it is, a series of forms,
repetons varied as the flight of

diptera and hymenoptera connecting
the dotted lines, less than

the length of my house, longer than several strides,
long enough to breathe and see –

in order for the world to have been formed again
this reality
in its current guise informs until

punctuation – the indicative,
the signal of return, a venture

into the contiguous world –

Formation of the Black Arrow

Paul Klee, Pedagogical Sketchbook, Section 40

Days which, having passed, cannot be.

Remembered, hours and minutes.

Likewise the same, now and again.

The minutes, the spaces between them.

And between those, and between those.

Thinking about what has or has not been.

Apprehension of what will or will not be.

The black pigment in my hand.

The white page.

The pressed fibers; the burnt, bound ash.

The minutes, the spaces.

Onto, into, down, a direction now, as if to bone.

Notes and Acknowledgments

The sections of this book represent a rough chronology, as well as an approximate topography: Section 1, 1991–1994, Vancouver Island and various camps between Canada and California; Section 2, 1994–1997, Marin County, California; Section 3, 1997–2000, Northern California, Nevada, and Eastern Oregon; Section 4, 2000–2003, the Lower Columbia River; and Section 5, 2004-2006, mostly an unnamed region of the interior.

p. 4 *Velella velella* is a small, deep blue hydroid, a jellyfish-like creature often found drying in masses on ocean beaches of western North America. It normally travels at the surface with the aid of a somewhat rigid triangular sail held above buoyant float tissue. Individuals with two types of sails that are mirror images of each other exist in a population – they are thus pushed in opposite directions by the wind.

pp. 12,13 Waldport and Likely are "triggering towns," in the sense of Richard Hugo's essay of the same name. "That silo you never saw until today was yours the day you were born."

p. 14 *In the Last Oak Meadows.* Garry, or Oregon white, oak *(Quercus garryana)* has its northernmost range on southern Vancouver Island. When this poem was written in 1991, the Vancouver Island subspecies of the Large Marble (now called Island Marble) was considered extinct, and the British Columbia Ministry of Environment was preparing to spray the oak habitat with *Bacillus thuringensis* to eradicate a suspected appearance of gypsy moths. There was and is considerable concern that many other lepidopterans would also be adversely affected by the biocide. In 1998, the presumed extinct butterfly was rediscovered on San Juan Island, between Vancouver Island and the Washington Mainland.

p. 18 *Letter from Saanich.* This epistolary poem and those from Wawona and Clatsop are also indebted to the example of Richard Hugo *(31 Letters and 13 Dreams).*

p. 31 Written on the occasion of one of many floods in northern California during the El Niño year, 1996.

p. 46 After an actual Sheriff's Report in *The Point Reyes Light.*

p. 55 *Elanus leucurus* is the White-tailed Kite, a graceful, gull-like bird of prey of coastal and interior California (recently seen to be extending its range to Oregon and southern Washington state). It locates its small prey by hovering.

p. 73 A*cquistorium* is a name given (John Walker, *Lectures on Geology,* 1779) to the short interval of stasis between ebb and flood tides.

p. 77 *Grebe.* The Pied-Billed Grebe, *Podylimbus podiceps,* can, with the aid of its adjustable air bladder, dive or sink with amazing speed. See *Letter from Clatsop,* p. 81.

p. 78 *Argumentum Odonatum. Naiads, instars,* and *tenerals* refer to stages of the incomplete metamorphosis of dragonflies (family Odonata), which spend most of their lives on the muddy bottom of bodies of water, then a shorter life of flight during summer.

p. 79 *Energy and Matter at South Jetty.* *Spisula californica* is the small surf clam, with a fragile whitish shell marked by concentric undulations on the beaks.

p. 84 *Vespers.* European Starlings *(Sturnus vulgaris)* gather from all directions in the evening along the Columbia River waterfront in Astoria.

p. 86 *Aria – Heart Music.* I sat with my father during his echocardiogram.

p. 88 My great-uncle Herman A. Darms photographed the Yukon/ Alaska gold rush in 1900. *The Steamer* Casca *Encounters Heavy Ice Enroute to Whitehorse* is one of his surviving original prints.

p. 91 *Ultima Ratio Regum* was written on September 15, 2001, at the estuary near the mouth of the Skagit River (also known as the Skagit Sea) in northern Washington state, while reconnaissance aircraft from nearby Whidbey Island Naval Air Station circled low overhead.

p. 93 *First Record of Field Crescent in Gray's Harbor County.* This butterfly was discovered and documented by poet and ecologist Bill Yake and myself, in a new extension of its range in Olympic National Forest, on August 13, 2002. On the same day we found a Red Admirable, and on the following day, a California Tortoiseshell, both also first records in the county.

p. 99 *Hermes and Sol.* "In alchemical writings the word 'Mercurius' is used with a very wide range of meaning, to denote not only the chemical name mercury or quicksilver, Mercury

(Hermes) the god, and Mercury the planet, but also – and primarily – the secret 'transforming substance' which is at the same time the 'spirit' in-dwelling in all living creatutes." (C.G. Jung, *Psychology and Alchemy*)

p. 100 *Descriptus.* *Volvox* is a genus of green near-microscopic organisms with flagella that form spherical colonies, marvellous under the microscope to a freshman biology student.

p. 106 *Composition.* The marginal notes are from an essay on the importance of color in his music by Olivier Messiaen.

p. 107 *Gift of the Grand Gesture.* An *enso* is the circle of infinity in Zen calligraphy. "It sometimes forms a moon, sometimes a rice cake." (John Stevens, *Sacred Calligraphy of the East*).

p. 108 A *netsuke* is traditionally a small carved toggle used to attach a small container to a kimono sash.

p. 113 *First Month, Fifteenth Day.* On January 9, 2006, Captain Kevin Murray failed to make the transfer from the cargo ship *Dry Beam* to the Columbia Bar Pilot vessel *Chinook* at night in 18 foot seas and 25 mile per hour winds. His body was found on a Washington beach two days later. This poem is written in the general Japanese form of *haibun,* a short prose piece with interspersed verse, or *hokku.*

Thanks to my fellowship of poets at large, especially Bill Yake, Devon Vose, James Mantooth, Nancy Cherry, and Chris Carless; to my teachers, especially Dolores Fischer, Saul Weisberg, Robert Michael Pyle, Marvin Bell, Pattiann Rogers, Robert Hass, Jane Hirshfield, and Kim Addonizio; to my writing students at Glenlyon-Norfolk School in Victoria, B.C. and Marin Primary and Middle School in Larkspur, California; to those who have supported the process, including Paul Alcala, Valerie Straw, Lisa Darms, Susan Darms, Richard Olafson, Matt Fair, Jim Andrews, Christine Colasurdo, Kathleen Lanphier and Oliver's Books, Joyce Jenkins and *Poetry Flash,* the Marin Poetry Center, and the Olympic Poetry Network; to all those in writing groups and workshops with whom I have practiced over the years in Victoria, Port Townsend, the San Francisco Bay Area, and the Lower Columbia River; to all the contributors and correspondents to my literary magazine *convolvulus* over most of the life of the body of poems in this book; and above all to Christi Payne, my compass rose, *mia cor.*

This book was designed by the Poet at Duckburg,
the float house on the tidal John Day River near Astoria.
It is set in Robert Slimbach's neo-humanist text face Minion,
and printed by Lightning Source in Tennessee.

www.ingramcontent.com/pod-product-compliance
Lightning Source LLC
LaVergne TN
LVHW091004080826
845145LV00003B/1114

* 9 7 8 1 8 8 7 8 5 3 2 2 4 *